Holy Saturday

*An Easter Chancel
Drama in Three Acts*

R. Kevin Mohr

CSS Publishing Company, Inc.
Lima, Ohio

HOLY SATURDAY

For more information about CSS Publishing Company resources, visit our website at www.csspub.com, email us at csr@csspub.com, or call (800) 241-4056.

ISBN-13: 978-0-7880-2673-7
ISBN-10: 0-7880-2673-9

PRINTED IN USA

*To my wife, Debbie, for all her love, support,
and encouragement*

*To the people of
English Lutheran Church, Bluffton, Ohio,
who first helped bring "Holy Saturday" to life*

Production Notes

Characters with speaking parts:
John
James, brother of John
Bartholomew
Mary, mother of Jesus
Philip *(may be combined with role of Bartholomew)*
Andrew
Peter
Mary Magdalene
Mary Joses
Matthew
Thomas
Mary Clopas *(may be played by the same person portraying Jesus' mother, Mary)*
Joana *(may be played by the same person portraying Mary Joses)*

This drama can also be done as a "readers' theater" with limited staging. The number of actors could be reduced by combining the roles of Philip and Bartholomew and by eliminating Thaddeus, James the son of Alphaeus, and Judas completely, as they have no speaking parts.

All of the action takes place in the "upper room." Very little furniture is needed for the set: a few low stools or benches and a large table. All entrances and exits are made through one door either stage left or right, but not center stage.

Act One

As the play begins, the disciples of Jesus are dispersed about the room: they are Peter, James, the brother of John, Matthew, Andrew, Bartholomew, Philip, Thomas, Thaddeus, James, the son of Alphaeus, and Judas [not Iscariot]. Peter is off in a corner, seated on the floor. Matthew and Andrew watch him with deep concern. The others are scattered about the room, singly or in groups of two, seated or standing. They are all stricken with grief and/or shock. (There is the sudden sound of knocking on the door. All are frozen with fear; no one approaches the door. The knocking is heard again and then a voice.)

John: Open up! It's me — John! Mary's with me too. Let us in!

(James opens the door just wide enough for John and Mary, the mother of Jesus, to enter.)

James: Hurry inside! *(He takes a quick look outside, then shuts and bolts the door. The rest, excepting Peter, gather around John and Mary.)*

Bartholomew: *(to James)* Were they followed?

James: No! I don't think so.

Mary: *(with extreme weariness, to John)* Thank you, John. I think I would like to lie down for a while. I am so tired.

John: *(gently)* Of course, Mary. Andrew?

7

(Andrew comes across to Mary and leads her off to one side. He makes her comfortable on the floor. When she is a safe distance away, James begins to scold John.)

James: What do you think you were doing bringing her here, John? You might have been followed!

John: *(not comprehending)* What...?

James: Use your head! They got him and now they're probably after us. You could have led them right to us.

John: I don't know if anyone followed us and, quite frankly, after what I've seen today, I don't really care.

James: What are you saying? You saw what they did to him. Do you want the same to happen to us? Our lives are in danger and you brought *her* here!

John: Are our lives all that important anymore? Besides, where else could I have taken her? Think of Mary, man — she is — was — his mother!

James: And we... we were his closest friends. Oh, I'm sorry, John! Nothing makes any sense now. I don't know what I'm saying. I... I... I'm so scared!

John: I know, brother. We all are. I was so scared at Golgotha that I almost deserted Mary when she needed me most.

Bartholomew: What was it like... out there?

John: It was awful! I don't know how Mary was able to stand it. She's stronger than she looks. I tried to convince her beforehand that she shouldn't go because I knew it was going to be terrible but also because I was afraid we might be arrested. I didn't want to see him suffer, and I didn't want to end up on a cross myself. We got to the hill just after the Roman soldiers had finished crucifying Jesus and two criminals. I'm glad we missed the actual nailing to the crosses. Just hearing the hammer-blows was bad enough! The three men suffered terribly as they struggled to keep their weight off of the nails, but it was a useless struggle.

No one — no one should have to die that way! The pain! The cries and moans! The tears! Thinking about it now almost makes sick to my stomach again.

James: How did you bear it, John?

John: I couldn't. I was sure that at any moment one of the scribes or Pharisees there would recognize me. As my fear increased I began to feel sick to my stomach. The panic and nausea grew so strong that I had decided to turn and run as far away as possible from that accursed spot.

But just at that moment — as if he knew I was about to desert his mother, even as I deserted him — right then, Jesus looked down at Mary and said to her, "Woman, there is your son." And then he looked directly at me and said, "There is your mother."

After that, when I quit thinking only of myself and started thinking of Mary and what she was going through, I was able to stand it. I was still afraid and sick but his words, his confidence in me gave me the strength necessary to stay with her. We stood there together until the end.

Bartholomew: You mean he's dead?

9

John: Yes.

James: But how can that be? He's only been out there for... for just a few hours. We all know that some poor wretches have lasted — if that's the word for it — up to three days on a cross! You must be mistaken, John. He can't possibly be dead already!

John: I'm afraid it's true: He *is* dead. I... *(gestures toward Mary)* we saw him breathe his last breath. But you're right, John, it *is* hard to believe that someone so... so vital and energetic could succumb to the cross so quickly. *(He pauses in reflection.)* We could hardly keep up with him in our walks through Galilee and Judea....

You know, the more I think about his death, the stranger it all seems. I mean... it was almost as if he surrendered to death rather than — oh, I don't know! Without him everything is so unclear!

Bartholomew: Maybe he just fainted?

John: No, Bartholomew. There's no doubt about his death now. He was dead even before the soldiers came — they didn't have to break his legs so that he would die before the Sabbath. What hypocrisy! We mustn't mar the Sabbath, especially the Passover Sabbath, with an innocent corpse hanging on the cross for all the world to see!

The soldiers broke the legs of the two thieves, but when they came to Jesus he was already dead. I saw one of them spear him in the side just to make sure. There is absolutely no doubt: he is gone.

Philip: So, it is all finally finished.

John: I don't know, Philip. I can't exactly explain it but after watching Jesus die there's something inside me that says, "This can't be all there is. There must be something more!"

Philip: He's dead, John, you said so yourself. How could there be anything more?

John: I don't know... I'm not sure....

(Andrew approaches John.)

Andrew: John, I'm very worried about Peter!

John: Why, what's wrong with him, Andrew?

Andrew: That's just it. We don't know. Matthew found him wandering the streets in a daze this morning. No one had seen him since the night before. Matthew brought him here. Peter just sits there in the corner, muttering over and over again, "I'll never deny you, Lord. I'll never deny you." And then he cries. I've *never* seen him cry before! Could you try to talk with him?

John: Of course! *(They walk over to Peter and John kneels down beside him. He takes a cup from Matthew and offers it to Peter.)* Here, Peter! Drink this. Take heart, Peter, it's over now.

Peter: Huh? What... *(Peter looks up slowly and then recognizes John.)* Oh, it's you, John. What did you say?

John: It's all over, Peter. He isn't suffering anymore.

Peter: All over? Not suffering, you say? Is that supposed to help? Is it? And is it really finished, John? Perhaps his suffering is over, but not ours. And not mine. Oh, how I wish that my agony could be ended so quickly! But no! I don't even have as much courage as Judas did.

John: Don't say that, Peter! That wasn't courage Judas showed when he took his own life — just fear and despair and... and pride. Yes, pride! His pride blinded him to the fact that God could forgive him even for the heinous thing he had done.

We may never be able to forgive Judas but you know as well as I do that Jesus would have forgiven him on the spot if he had repented. But no! He took the easy way out.

Peter: Easy? *You* can say that, John. *You* were at the cross. *You* didn't desert him. *You* didn't deny ever knowing him. But *I* let him down when he needed me most!

Andrew: But, Peter, we all did that. You bear no more blame than the —

Peter: No! I do because I'm Peter, the Rock! Isn't — wasn't that his nickname for me? Some "rock" I turned out to be! I was so disgusted with myself after I ran from Gethsemane. So I followed him to the high priest's home. I thought that maybe I could somehow help him. I wanted to prove his prediction about me wrong. But the longer I stayed in that courtyard, the more scared I became. It was dangerous there and I became more convinced that his enemies were actually going to have him condemned to death! And then —

John: Peter, why —

Peter: Do you know at the supper right here in this room — when was it, just the other night? — when he told me that I would betray him three times before morning, I almost hit him! Not because his words hurt me and I thought he was wrong, but... because I knew he was right... he was right... he was right.... Leave me alone!

Andrew: Peter!

John: Let him be for now, Andrew.

(The group moves away from Peter.)

Andrew: But what are we going to do, John? I can't bear to see him like this!

John: We'll just have to be patient for now and wait. Peter is strong. You'll see. I'm sure he will come out of it soon.

Andrew: And what if he doesn't?

(Any reply is interrupted by sudden knocking on the door. All are frozen with fear, staring at the door. The knocking comes again, followed by a hushed voice.)

Mary Magdalene: Peter! James! John! Are you in there? Please let us in!

John: It's Mary Magdalene! Let her in.

(One of the disciples opens the door and two women enter: Mary Magdalene [Mary M.] and Mary Joses [Mary J.]. Mary M. is in shock and speaks her lines with a weary, emotionless voice.)

Mary M.: We cannot stay long. We want to go and anoint the Lord's body for burial. But we need some money to buy the spices before the Sabbath begins.

Mary J.: May we have some money from the treasury?

James: *(to Mary M.)* Do you think that is wise, Mary? They saw you at Golgotha; none of us should be out now. In fact, they may have followed you here.

Mary M.: I don't care. What does it matter if they kill me — if they kill all of us now that he is gone? *(with some emotion)* I want to — no! I *need* to do this! It is the least I can do for him after what he did for me.

John: Where is he being buried?

Mary J.: Nicodemus and Joseph of Arimathea got permission from Pilate to bury the Master in a tomb that Joseph owns near Golgotha.

Andrew: Well, at least he'll have a decent burial.

Mary J.: Only if we can buy the spices! Will you give us some money or not? We must hurry!

(Mary, the mother of Jesus, has awakened during the previous discussion.)

Mary: I would like to go with you.

Mary J.: Certainly, Mary... if you're sure?

Mary: I want to go.

Mary J.: And you men? *(There is no response.)* Then can we at least have some money? The Sabbath is almost here!

Matthew: Of course! Of course! *(He removes the bag from his cincture.)* There isn't very much left now.... *(He hands the bag to her.)* Here, take it all!

Mary J.: Thank you! It will help. We must go!

(The three women begin to leave. As Mary M. reaches the door, Matthew calls out.)

Matthew: Shalom! God be with you!

(Mary M. pauses in the door and turns toward Matthew.)

Mary M.: After what happened this afternoon do you really expect God to be with us? Do you actually think God cares?

(She exits and pulls the door shut behind her.)

End of Act One

Act Two

(The scene opens with the disciples still in the "upper room." It is very early in the morning. Andrew takes a cup over to Peter, who is still sitting on the floor in one corner of the room. Andrew kneels down and offers the cup to Peter.)

Andrew: Peter! Peter! Here, drink this — you've had nothing since Friday! *(There is no reaction from Peter. Andrew stands up and angrily bangs the cup down on the table.)* It just isn't fair! It just isn't fair!

John: What? What was that, Andrew?

Andrew: Why is all this happening to us? Why did he do this to us? Why? Why?

John: Why did *he* do this to us? Who are you talking about?

Andrew: *(angrily)* Jesus! Who else? Why did he ever call us together — the most mismatched group of men... no, not men... eleven fools and... and a devil! Yes, that's it: eleven fools and a devil following what all over the country? An illusion called the kingdom of God? A fantasy? A fake or just another fool like us?

We suffered ridicule, cold nights without a proper bed, and days without food for what? For nothing! Nothing but dashed hopes, shattered dreams, and the constant fear that every footstep we hear could be the soldiers coming for us — to nail us to our crosses!

And look at Peter. Peter, who could haul in a full net of fish almost single-handedly, cowering in a corner, jabbering away to himself like an idiot! We may have deserted Jesus, but if this is all there is to his kingdom of God then his betrayal of us is even worse, and... and... I hate him for it!

(There is complete, shocked silence at the end of Andrew's outburst. Finally John responds slowly and gently.)

John: Andrew, you can't really mean that! *He* never failed us; *we* failed him! I'm not sure we ever fully understood who he was, what he said and did, and what he wanted us to be and do. Maybe if we had understood better none of this would have happened. Maybe we're missing something.

Andrew: Oh, I'd like to hope so, John, but all I know now is how I feel. And how I feel toward him at this moment makes me feel ashamed — it makes me hate myself even more than I hate him for what he has done to us!

(Andrew breaks down with emotion. After a brief silence, John continues.)

John: But what about the good times we had together? You're right, Andrew, there were a few hunger-filled days, there were stones, insults, and curses hurled at us. We did spend cold nights out under the stars, huddled together for warmth. But there also were hours spent joking, laughing, and talking around a fire on the beach.... Remember when the fish and bread multiplied before our eyes and that huge crowd was fed?

Bartholomew: And not just once, but it happened twice!

Matthew: Or how about the time he turned water into wine...

Philip: Or when he walked on the water!

Matthew: We all thought he was a ghost!

Thomas: We didn't just imagine all of that, did we?

Matthew: The shocked looks on the Pharisees' faces were real enough when he answered their trick questions.

Philip: His jokes were the best and I could have listened to his stories about the kingdom of God all day long.

James: I'm still not sure I understood them all. But I did get the point when he would put us in our places. He wasn't at all shy about doing that when we needed it, was he, John?

John: No, he wasn't! But the memory that is clearest in my mind is when he yelled, "Lazarus, come out!" And then Lazarus walked out of the tomb alive and well. I'll never forget that moment!

(There is silence while they all contemplate the past. The silence is broken unexpectedly by Peter.)

Peter: But memories aren't enough. He is dead. Who will call him out of the tomb as he called Lazarus? You, Thomas? Perhaps you, Philip? What about you, John? Just as I thought — none of us will dare. Without him we are nothing. We need *him* — not memories.

(There is a sudden pounding on the door and the sound of a voice.)

Mary M.: Oh, let me in! Let me in!

John: It's Mary Magdalene!

(He opens the door for her; she staggers in, sobbing.)

Mary M.: Oh Peter! John! They've taken the Lord's body away!

(Peter springs up immediately on hearing Mary's words, looks at John, then rushes out the door, followed by John and the weeping Mary M. Philip shuts the door behind them.)

Philip: They've killed him! Isn't that enough for them? Why can't they leave him alone? Why can't they leave us alone with our grief?

Matthew: *(to himself)* None of this had to happen...

Andrew: What was that, Matthew?

Matthew: Why didn't I say something? I could see it all falling apart.

Andrew: You're not making any sense at all, Matthew.

Matthew: Maybe I could have prevented all of this from happening.

Thomas: What do you mean?

Matthew: I knew that Judas had gone bad. I saw it start to happen when Jesus refused to allow the crowd to make him king after he fed the five thousand. Judas understood Jesus even less than rest of us... or maybe he understood him better than we did. But it doesn't matter now. What mattered was that Judas became disillusioned with Jesus and began to steal from the money bag.

(There is a general outcry of astonishment at this announcement.)

Thomas: How do you know that?

Matthew: Remember, I was a crooked tax-collector once — no more corrupt than most, but still a crooked one. Believe me, I know when the purse has a hole in it!

Thomas: But why didn't we notice any of this?

Matthew: Because you're all simple Galilean fishermen. You wouldn't know corruption if it stepped up to you and slapped you in the face! You've probably never seen the disease of real corruption at work in a person before. I knew the symptoms. But still, I did nothing! I said nothing!

You know, I believe Jesus knew that Judas was a thief all along too.... Why did he call Judas to be one of us? Why? Well, it doesn't matter now.

Philip: Please stop! I don't want to hear anymore. It only makes things worse!

Matthew: No, Philip, I won't be quiet! That's our whole problem: we've been far too quiet when we should have spoken out. We said we believed in Jesus' great commandments: to love God and to love our neighbors. But did any of us ever really make an attempt to love Judas at all? Most of us didn't even bother to talk with him unless we wanted some money from him. No, we ignored him. We made jokes about him behind his back. And now he's dead.

Andrew: Matthew, please —

Matthew: We said that we believed in Jesus and his vision of the kingdom. We all agreed with Peter when he said he would lay down his life for the Master. Yet one short hour later we all deserted him in the garden! Did any of us speak in his defense before the Sanhedrin? No! We were silent. Well, our silence killed him as much as the cross did!

(Once again there is the sound of pounding on the door. Two women's voices — Mary, wife of Clopas [Mary C.] and Joana — are heard.)

Mary C. and Joana: Let us in! Oh, let us in!

James: It's Joana and Clopas' wife!

(James opens the door. The women burst into the room.)

Mary C.: He's alive! He's alive!

Joana: Yes, the angels told us that he's alive! Praise God!

James: What?

Andrew: How can that be?

Thomas: What are you talking about? What angels?

Joana: We went to the tomb early this morning to finish anointing the Master's body. We were supposed to meet Mary Magdalene there.

Mary C.: When we got to the tomb it was still quite dark, but we could see that the stone blocking the entrance had been rolled away...

Joana: Our first thought was that his body had been stolen. We were terribly frightened, but we had to know what had happened so we peeked into the tomb.

Mary C.: It was empty...

Joana: At least, we thought so at first. Then we saw an angel...

Mary C.: Or maybe two — we're not sure...

Joana: They were sitting on the ledge where the body should have been. We could barely stand to look at the angels — the light was so bright! They told us that he is alive!

Mary C.: We were terrified and happy at the same time!

Joana: Isn't it wonderful? He's alive!

James: Did you see him?

Mary C.: Jesus? Well, no... not exactly.

Thomas: *(skeptical)* Uh huh!

Joana: But we saw the angels! They told us he was alive and then they told us to come straight here and tell you all the good news!

Thomas: But you didn't actually see Jesus?

Joana: No, Thomas. We didn't actually *see* Jesus. But the tomb *is* empty!

Thomas: Which doesn't necessarily prove anything. Let's face it, the evidence is not exactly overwhelming: You admit that you haven't seen Jesus. You talk about seeing angels and yet you can't agree on how many! Well, I'm not going to get my hopes up based on a wild story from two excitable women who can't even get their facts straight.

Joana: But it's true, Thomas! You others — you believe us, don't you?

James: Well, Joana... Thomas makes a pretty good case! We all have been through a lot in the last few days. We all want him to be alive so badly that... Well, why don't we wait and see what Peter and John have to say?

Mary C.: Oh — you are all impossible! What's wrong with you? Don't you want him to be alive? Or is it that your pride is hurt at not being the first to know? He is alive!

Joana: Come on, Mary. We don't have time to waste here. The rest of the women need to be told the wonderful news!

(The two women leave. There is an embarrassed silence among the disciples, finally broken by Andrew.)

Andrew: What if the women are right? What if he really is alive? Could it be true, James?

James: I don't think so, Andrew. I think Thomas is probably right: they just got excited when they saw that the tomb was empty. Who knows? They may have even gone to the wrong tomb in the early morning darkness. Let's see what Peter has to say.

(A man's voice is heard offstage.)

Andrew: Listen! Here they come now. I think I hear John's voice.

*(He goes to the door and opens it a crack to peer out, then opens it wider to admit Peter and John. The door is pushed shut but **not** closed completely. John has been talking excitedly to Peter. On entering the room, he breaks off and makes an announcement.)*

John: The tomb is empty!

Peter: *(looking around)* Where is Mary Magdalene?

James: Isn't she with you? We thought she had followed you back to the tomb.

Andrew: What did you find?

John: I arrived at the tomb first but was afraid to go in. But not Peter! Without even a pause he ran right past me and stepped into the tomb. I followed him. The linen cloths that had covered the body were on the ledge where the body had lain. And off to one side, neatly rolled up, was the napkin used for covering the head. Obviously the body has not been stolen!

Peter: We can't be sure of that, John.

John: Come on, Peter! Grave robbers don't take the time to unwrap the body and neatly roll up the napkin! No, there can only be one explanation...

Matthew: And that is?

John: He's alive!

(At these words Peter moves away quickly.)

Andrew: That's exactly what the women said!

John: Which women?

James: Clopas' wife and Joana. They must have arrived at the garden shortly after Mary Magdalene and then they rushed back here with a not-too-coherent story about an angel or angels telling them that Jesus is alive.
    But that can't be true, unless... unless you were mistaken, John, about him being dead in the first place?

John: No, not a chance! He was dead. I'm sure of it.

Philip: Then... the women are right? That's just not possible!

John: I don't know... I don't understand it at all. But I believe the women. I think he *is* alive! What about you, Peter?

Peter: Please don't ask me that question! I don't know what to think. Part of me wants to believe. Part of me cries, "Oh please, let it be true! Let me hear his voice again!" But... the other part of me isn't so sure — if he is alive, how can I ever face him again? How could I ever look in those eyes again? And what if it's all a big hoax, a trick to trap us all? No one has seen him yet. Maybe it's all a lie or we're all dreaming. I'm... I'm not very sure of reality anymore.... *(with desperation)* I wish I could believe, John! I really do, but I don't dare! If only someone had seen him... if only we could be sure...

(There is the sound of running feet and then Mary M. bursts through the door — left unbolted after Peter and John's entrance. She is breathless and barely able to gasp out her message.)

Mary M.: I have seen the Lord!

End of Act Two

Act Three

(The scene takes place in the "upper room." The room is filled with all of the disciples and the women. They are all arranged around the large table in the center of the room. Peter stands center stage, behind the table. He takes a flat loaf of bread in his hands and speaks.)

[**Production Note:** *If the play is performed in a congregational setting it may be appropriate to have a clergyperson as one of the characters at the table "presiding" over the meal and then have the actors serve Holy Communion to the assembly before the hymn of praise referred to below.*]

Peter: Remember, friends, how on the night when he was betrayed our Lord took bread, and when he had given thanks he broke it and gave it to us, saying: "Take and eat; this is my body, given for you. Do this for the remembrance of me."

(Peter breaks the bread and it is shared with the group. He then takes a cup of wine in his hands.)

Then he took the cup, and after giving thanks he gave it to us, saying: "Take and drink. This cup is the new covenant in my blood, shed for you and for all people for the forgiveness of sin. Do this for the remembrance of me."

(The cup is then shared with the group. [The congregation may be communed at this point.]When all have received, a short hymn of praise is sung, followed by a moment of silence. Matthew is the first to speak.)

Matthew: We surely have much for which to be thankful this Pentecost!

Bartholomew: But you know, even after all that has happened in the past month, it is still hard to believe that Jesus is alive.

Andrew: Especially now that he is gone again! What was it, less than two weeks ago that we saw him last?

Philip: And now once again we don't know what to do or where to go. This waiting is driving me crazy — we should be doing something!

Thomas: We've got to be patient, Philip. But regardless of how long we have to wait now, I know one thing for sure.

Philip: What's that, Thomas?

Thomas: The next time the women tell us they have seen or heard something, I for one am going to believe them — even without seeing for myself!

(There is general laughter at Thomas' statement.)

Mary M.: *(with a laugh)* And well you should, Thomas! But I really don't blame any of you for not believing us at first. Why, I could hardly believe it myself when I heard him say my name in the garden. I don't think I shall ever hear a more beautiful sound than his voice saying, "Mary." Every time someone says my name now I turn quickly, expecting it to be him!

(Mary M., Peter, James, and John move downstage apart from the rest of the group. The others gather upstage around Matthew.)

James: I know just what you mean, Mary. It is impossible to concentrate on fishing anymore. I keep looking up to see if he is preparing a meal for us on the beach.

John: *(to Peter)* You're very quiet today, Peter. Is anything wrong?

Peter: No, not really... I've just been thinking.

Mary M.: About what?

Peter: Well... I'm ashamed to admit it now, but though I didn't act like it at the time, I actually did believe Mary when she told us that she had seen the Lord.

John: What!?

Peter: *(to John)* Yes, it's true. *(to Mary M.)* I'm sorry, Mary! I truly am, and I ask for your forgiveness...

Mary M.: Of course, Peter, I forgive you! But... but why didn't you say something at the time?

Peter: Because I was afraid! *(pause)* I didn't want to face him after what I had done. I was so ashamed of myself that I almost didn't want him to be alive again!
But then, after we knew that he had risen from the dead — after we had seen him here in this room — I was being pulled in two opposite directions: On the one hand I was so glad to see him that I couldn't bear to be away from his side.

At the same time I felt so terribly uncomfortable around him. I didn't know what to do or what to say!

John: I know. I could see that you were struggling with something.

Peter: *He* was alive, but in a real sense... *I* was dead! My pride was standing in the way of my receiving the forgiveness I so desperately needed. It was pretty awful there for a while.

James: Yes, I can imagine that it was. But you seem... better, more at peace now. What happened?

Peter: Well, remember that day when he made breakfast for us on the beach at the Sea of Galilee?

James: Yes....

Peter: After breakfast that day, Jesus and I took a walk along the beach. We walked in silence for a long time. To be quite truthful, I was a nervous wreck! You see, that was the first time I had been alone with Jesus since his resurrection.

Then suddenly, out of the blue, Jesus asked me, "Simon, son of John, do you love me more than these?" I told him, "Yes, Lord, you know that I love you." He replied, "Feed my lambs."

We walked on in silence and then he asked me again, "Simon, son of John, do you love me?" Perplexed by his repeated question, I told him again, "Yes, Lord, you know that I love you!" He answered again, "Tend my sheep."

I was nearly out of my mind when he asked me a third time, "Simon, son of John, do you love me?" I cried out to him, "Lord, you know everything! You know that I love you!" And once again he said, "Feed my sheep."

At that moment, somewhere off in the distance I think I heard a cock crow — and then it hit me! Then I understood!

John: *(remembering)* "Before the cock crows you will deny me three times!"

Peter: Yes, John. I found out then that forgiveness is hard. It hurts the forgiver and the forgiven. But it is a good hurt... like when you have a broken bone reset. The pain is terrible, but it is necessary if any healing is to take place. The alternative is to be a cripple for the rest of your life.

God's forgiveness is severe but merciful — it is still hard to believe that Jesus had to die for us — but we can't live without forgiveness! Now, because he is alive and I've been forgiven, I'm ready to face whatever it is he has in mind for us.

Mary M.: I'm so happy for you, Peter!

(loud laughter breaks out from the other group)

Peter: Let's see what story Matthew is telling this time. Wait! *(There is the sound of a rushing wind.)* Listen! What's that noise?

(All freeze with hands and faces raised. Lights out.)

The Beginning